*Ashley L. Allen*

# Exclusively
# WHITE HOUSE
## TRIVIA
### by Anthony S. Pitch

D1115067

Mino Publications
Potomac, Md.

Published by

Mino Publications
9009 Paddock Lane
Potomac, Md. 20854

Library of Congress Catalog Card
No. 98-65048

ISBN 0-931719-10-0

Printed in the United States of America

For Marion, Michael and Nomi

# QUESTIONS

1. Where is the artist's mistake in George Washington's portrait in the East Room?

2. Which First Ladies died close to the White House?

3. When did British troops burn the White House?

4. Why did skinflint Calvin Coolidge head for the cellar?

5. What wood is used for the Lincoln Bed?

6. Who changed the official name from Executive Mansion to the White House?

7. What's the link between the White House and the *Titanic*?

8. Who had to be house-trained before moving into the Clinton White House?

9. What prize did James Hoban select after winning the design for the White House?

1

# ANSWERS

1. Part of the title of a painted book under the table reads United Sates.

2. Dolley Madison at her home on Lafayette Square and Abigail Fillmore in the Willard Hotel.

3. On the night of Wednesday, 24 August 1814.

4. To count the contents of a barrel of apples he got as a gift.

5. Rosewood.

6. Theodore Roosevelt in 1901.

7. President Taft's top aide, Archie Butt, drowned when it sank in 1912.

8. Buddy, the president's chocolate-colored labrador pup.

9. A medal instead of the optional $500.

10. Why did sheep graze on the lawns in World War 1?

11. When were gas lights installed?

12. What did alert security agents find in a fountain pen sent to President Hoover?

13. What souvenirs did British Admiral George Cockburn take before burning the White House?

14. Who would be entitled to move in on the death of the president and vice president?

15. Who planted the magnolia tree to the left of the south portico?

16. How long did President Truman live away from the White House during renovations?

17. What made First Lady Barbara Bush shriek at the swimming pool?

18. How did Edith Wilson's right arm get skinned raw?

# ANSWERS

10. To free grass-cutting laborers for military service.

11. 1848.

12. Explosive materials in the rubber ink container.

13. A hat and a cushion.

14. The Speaker of the House of Representatives.

15. President Andrew Jackson.

16. Three years and four months, until March 1952.

17. There was a rat in the water.

18. Every time she shook hands her arm rubbed against roses woven into her dress.

19. How many foreign languages did President Thomas Jefferson speak?

20. What did opera singer Leontyne Price sing during Pope John Paul II's White House visit?

21. Which country supplied the craftsmen who cut and set the stone walls?

22. Abraham Lincoln was assassinated on this religious anniversary.

23. Where is the landing pad for Marine One - the president's helicopter?

24. President Theodore Roosevelt's daughter said this president was "a slob."

25. Which bachelor president appointed his niece as White House hostess?

26. Name the author of the words on the State Dining Room fireplace: *May none but honest and wise men ever rule under this roof.*

27. Which pew is the president's in St. John's Church, Lafayette Square?

## ANSWERS

19. Four—French, Italian, Greek and Latin.

20. The Lord's Prayer.

21. Scotland.

22. Good Friday, 1865.

23. On the south lawn.

24. Warren Harding.

25. James Buchanan.

26. President John Adams.

27. Number 54, with a brass plaque reading *President's Pew.*

28. When was parachute silk used for curtains?

29. How did the Queens' Room get its name?

30. Which presidents died in the White House?

31. Where did Thomas Jefferson have his office?

32. Which president was carried mortally wounded out the front door?

33. This president's adult daughter reported seeing a transparent figure with a red robe in the Lincoln Bedroom.

34. Name the only president who later became a U.S. Senator.

35. Who sneaked a live pony upstairs?

36. Which first lady said she never went into the kitchen.

37. Who was the first president to have a seal of office?

28. When funds were low during the Eisenhower administration.

29. Because so many royals have slept there including the Queens of Great Britain, Greece, and the Netherlands.

30. William Henry Harrison in 1841 and Zachary Taylor in 1850.

31. In the section now used for the State Dining Room.

32. James Garfield, wounded by an assassin, died at his New Jersey cottage two weeks after leaving the White House.

33. Maureen Reagan.

34. Andrew Johnson.

35. Theodore Roosevelt's children, to comfort a sick sibling.

36. Lou Hoover.

37. Rutherford Hayes.

38. In which room did Woodrow Wilson collapse from a stroke in 1919?

39. Where did Abigail Adams hang her laundry?

40. Name the last Civil War veteran elected president.

41. What tragedy struck President-elect Andrew Jackson?

42. Who appointed Louis Tiffany to redecorate the White House?

43. Which two presidents took two strides every second when out walking?

44. Why did the original floors rot within a decade?

45. Whose portrait hung over the fireplace in Abraham Lincoln's office?

46. Why did Richard Nixon get rid of Lyndon Johnson's showerheads?

47. This president breakfasted and lunched with his pet Airedale.

# ANSWERS

38. In the bathroom next to his bed.

39. In the East Room.

40. William McKinley, elected 1896.

41. His beloved wife Rachel died and was buried Christmas eve 1828.

42. Chester Arthur, in 1882.

43. John Quincy Adams and Harry Truman.

44. The timber was unseasoned and exposed to rain before a roof went up.

45. Andrew Jackson's.

46. The controls were complex and water pressure almost bowled him over.

47. Warren Harding.

48. How did a Confederate widow get to live in the White House?

49. Why was the New Year's Day reception canceled in 1893?

50. When was water first piped in from the Potomac River?

51. How much did renovations cost 1949-52?

52. Where did Franklin Roosevelt keep his huge stamp collection?

53. When he was president the White House smelled of cigar smoke.

54. Which first couple entertained more than anyone else?

55. Why did President Truman add a controversial balcony on the south portico?

56. Which showbiz freak met Abraham Lincoln in the White House?

57. Who appointed one of his predecessors Chief Justice?

# ANSWERS

48. Emilie Helm was Mary Todd Lincoln's sister.

49. President Benjamin Harrison's grand-daughter was sick in the White House with scarlet fever.

50. 1859.

51. $5.8 million.

52. In his second floor study.

53. Ulysses S. Grant, who smoked 20 a day and died of throat cancer.

54. Herbert and Lou Hoover.

55. To enjoy the outdoors and to do away with unsightly summer awnings shading rooms on the south.

56. P.T. Barnum's star, "General" Tom Thumb.

57. Warren Harding appointed William Howard Taft.

58. In which room did Woodrow Wilson's daughter, Eleanor, marry in 1914?

59. Who kept memos to himself in his top hat?

60. George H.W. & George W. Bush belonged to this secret society.

61. An equestrian statue of this president is opposite the White House.

62. What was special about Sunday nights in the McKinley White House?

63. This president's favorite sports were duck-shooting and fishing.

64. When a ship's gun exploded on the Potomac River it killed this first lady's father.

65. Why did religious people turn on John Quincy Adams in 1835?

66. What did Washington City planner Pierre L'Enfant call the White House?

67. What are the origins of the White House press corps?

# ANSWERS

58. The Blue Room.

59. Abraham Lincoln.

60. Skull and Bones, at Yale.

61. Andrew Jackson, in Lafayette Square.

62. He sang hymns with a few friends after dinner.

63. Grover Cleveland.

64. Julia Gardiner Tyler.

65. They objected to his bringing a billiard table into the White House.

66. The Presidential Palace.

67. A reporter interviewed people entering and leaving the gate.

68. What was First Lady Edith Wilson nicknamed after allowing sheep on the lawns?

69. Who enjoyed putting his feet on the desk and smoking Havana cigars?

70. Why were President Hoover's desk draws thrown out the window?

71. Who was the first president not born a British subject?

72. This president had a habit of bowing to people he met.

73. Which president felt comfortable in clothes too big for him?

74. In which room did Richard Nixon kneel in prayer before resigning?

75. Why did President Benjamin Harrison string up a man in the White House?

76. Bad blood between President-elect Eisenhower and President Truman led to this incident on inauguration day.

# ANSWERS

68. Little Bo Peep.

69. President Calvin Coolidge.

70. To save their contents during a fire on Christmas eve 1929.

71. Martin Van Buren.

72. Thomas Jefferson.

73. Zachary Taylor.

74. The Lincoln Bedroom.

75. The intruder was struggling with door-keepers.

76. Eisenhower refused to get out of his car for coffee in the White House.

(77) Which 19th century vice-presidents took over on the death of the president?

78. What did President Clinton and daughter Chelsea traditionally do on Christmas eve?

79. Where did Thomas Jefferson dig a well?

80. Where did President McKinley sign the declaration of war against Spain in 1898?

81. Where did Woodrow Wilson sign the declaration of war against Germany in 1917?

82. What made the giant flag flutter over the White House on President Taft's 25th wedding anniversary.

83. Who looted the White House just before the British in 1814?

84. Who became a Virginia county supervisor of roads after leaving the White House?

# *ANSWERS*

77. John Tyler, Millard Fillmore, Andrew Johnson, Chester Arthur.

78. They shopped together for gifts.

79. Below the east wall.

80. In the cabinet room.

81. In the office of the White House usher.

82. Electric fans.

83. Some of the Washingtonians who had not fled.

84. John Tyler.

85. How did President Truman almost get run over on the way to the Oval Office?

86. Daniel Webster called her "the only permanent power in Washington."

87. Which president-elect promised to wear jeans in the White House?

88. Who walked her pet dog before sunrise?

89. What disconnected the first telephone link between the White House and the Treasury?

90. Who were derided for the animal designs on their porcelain dinner plates?

91. How did Pat Nixon favor blind visitors to the White House?

92. This president often hummed or sang a tune when he wasn't talking.

93. What gave President Reagan the chills one night in the White House?

# ANSWERS

85. He was crossing Pennsylvania Avenue from Blair House when a motorist braked hard.

86. Dolley Madison.

87. Jimmy Carter.

88. Barbara Bush.

89. An invited singer sang so loudly that he broke the telephone's sounding board.

90. Lucy and Ruthford Hayes.

91. Unlike the general public, they were allowed to touch the furniture.

92. Thomas Jefferson.

93. His dog barked and growled before backing away from the empty Lincoln Bedroom.

94. This president had boiled wheat and rye for breakfast because he hated factory brands.

95. Which first couple met for the first time in the White House?

96. Who always lunched on cottage cheese, A-1 Sauce, a tomato or onion, and butter-pecan ice cream?

97. Who wore torn slippers when receiving the Tunisian ambassador?

98. What made President Eisenhower so mad his neck turned red?

99. What was built next to the swimming pool for President Kennedy?

100. What was the cost of each of 20 spittoons in the East Room when Andrew Jackson was president?

101. When did thieves make off with guests' hats and coats during a White House reception?

102. What cuisine was distinctive at President Jefferson's dinners?

# ANSWERS

94. Calvin Coolidge.

95. Woodrow Wilson was a widower when his cousin brought Edith Galt to tea.

96. President Gerald Ford.

97. Thomas Jefferson, according to a contemporary British diplomat.

98. At a White House meeting a U.S. Senator said "the public be damned."

99. A gym.

100. $12.50

101. In 1861, four days after Abraham Lincoln's inauguration.

102. French.

103. Which president regularly bathed nude in the Potomac River?

104. On a hot day this 332 lb. president dressed in a kimono and said he looked like a Chinese idol.

105. When was the White House overrun by mobs gorging food and gulping punch?

106. Who left the White House to lay the cornerstone of the Washington Monument?

107. Who said California and Oregon were too far away to join the United States?

108. What made President Polk say something remarkable did not happen on 3 September 1846?

109. What parting gift did Lyndon and Lady Bird Johnson give the White House?

110. What is the oldest recorded tree on White House grounds?

# *ANSWERS*

103. John Quincy Adams.

104. William Howard Taft.

105. At the post-inaugural party for President Andrew Jackson in 1829.

106. President James Polk on 4 July 1848.

107. President-elect Zachary Taylor on the way to his inauguration.

108. Noone called at the White House to ask for a job.

109. A Children's Garden on the south lawn, with tiny furniture, goldfish pond and apple tree.

110. An elm planted by John Quincy Adams in 1826.

111. Guess the tab for Jackie Kennedy's clothes during a three month stretch in the White House?

112. Which president was given regular injections to fight allergies?

113. How did the 20th century honor First Lady Abigail Adams?

114. This first couple had 28 homes before moving into the White House.

115. What happened to the pilot who crashed a stolen plane on White House grounds in 1994?

116. This 21-year-old was nicknamed Yum-Yum when she married 49–year-old President Grover Cleveland.

117. This president began his day by taking acorns from his Oval Office desk to feed squirrels outside.

118. Who ordered the swimming pool walls painted with Virgin Islands' scenes?

119. In which room were top secret matters discussed during World War 2?

## *ANSWERS*

111. About $17,000.

112. Bill Clinton - allergic to weed and grass pollen, beef, milk, dust and mold.

113. With a commemorative 22 cent stamp showing her portrait and autograph.

114. Dwight and Mamie Eisenhower.

115. The unlicensed pilot died.

116. Frances Folsom.

117. Ronald Reagan.

118. President Kennedy.

119. The tightly-guarded Map Room.

# QUESTIONS

120. Who sweet-talked a billionaire into giving the White House his valuable portrait of Benjamin Franklin?

121. Which of the four trees planted by the Carters came from their own farm?

122. In which country was original White House designer James Hoban born?

123. How did John Quincy Adams busy himself on White House grounds?

124. When the newspapers arrived this president looked at the comics first.

125. Did Abraham Lincoln ever sleep in the Lincoln Bedroom?

126. Why did people donate knitting wool to the White House in 1919?

127. Why did President Thomas Jefferson prefer to ride horseback alone?

128. According to a typing error in this president's memoirs he brought household *gods* into the White House.

# *ANSWERS*

120. Jackie Kennedy charmed Walter Annenberg.

121. The loblolly pine.

122. County Kilkenny, Ireland.

123. Tending hundreds of herbs, flowers, shrubs, hedges, trees, and vegetables.

124. Ronald Reagan.

125. No. It got its name when the Hoovers moved in Lincoln's Bed.

126. Newspapers reported that President Wilson wore a torn sweater when meeting Belgian royalty.

127. He could meditate.

128. Herbert Hoover.

129. On the day of his assassination this president predicted his murder.

130. How long did experts say the mid-20th century renovations would last?

131. Why did John Quincy Adams break his tradition of not drinking toasts in the White House?

132. Who was the first president to win the Nobel Prize?

133. Why were the remains of White House planner Pierre L'Enfant exhumed 84 years later?

134. What was President James Buchanan's annual pay?

135. How heavy was the cheese on Washington's Birthday in Andrew Jackson's White House?

136. On what rare occasions did President McKinley leave the White House?

137. How many rooms were habitable for John Adams in 1800?

# ANSWERS

129. Abraham Lincoln, according to his bodyguard, William Crook.

130. Five hundred years.

131. To honor General Lafayette on the Frenchman's birthday, 6 September 1825.

132. Theodore Roosevelt in 1906 for helping to end the Russo-Japanese War.

133. For removal to Arlington National Cemetery in a belated tribute.

134. $25,000.

135. 1400 lbs.

136. For afternoon walks and drives.

137. Six.

138. When was the World War 1 suspension lifted on egg-rolling at the White House?

139. What happened when a visitor asked President Pierce if he could go through "your fine house."

140. When was the West Wing added?

141. Where is the tunnel allowing VIPs in and out of the White House unobserved?

142. Which first lady always sent flowers and food to sick staff?

143. Why did Jackie Kennedy visit seven years after her husband's assassination?

144. How did the Blue Room get its name?

145. Who sliced off the front lawn to make the grounds smaller?

146. When was the President's House already called the White House?

147. What is written on the label of an ax in the security command post?

# ANSWERS

138. 1921.

139. The president said it was the people's house and invited him in.

140. 1902.

141. Between the White House and Treasury basements.

142. Lou Hoover.

143. She was invited by the Nixons to view her official portrait.

144. President Martin Van Buren decorated it in blue in 1837.

145. President Thomas Jefferson.

146. Dolley Madison's friend, Phoebe Morris, wrote in 1812 that Democrats called it the White House.

147. *Key to the White House.*

148. Who was the only president not to live in the White House?

149. How was Robert E. Lee linked to White House building materials?

150. Which president ran out to jog and feast at a nearby McDonald's?

151. On which floor is the president's bedroom?

152. Why did George Washington insist on government agencies flanking the White House?

153. Guess the girth of President William Howard Taft.

154. Which president worked next door while an army major?

155. Which president went around switching off lights in empty rooms?

156. What did dignitaries do after the cornerstone was laid in 1792?

157. This first lady had a pet racoon.

# ANSWERS

148. George Washington.

149. His father, "Light-Horse Harry" Lee, supplied yellow poplar and white oak for woodwork.

150. President Clinton.

151. The second floor.

152. So they would be far from Congressional busybodies, who pestered civil servants when Philadelphia was the capital.

153. 54 inches.

154. Dwight Eisenhower, while working in the War department.

155. Lyndon Johnson.

156. They returned to the Fountain Inn, Georgetown, to feast and drink 16 formal toasts.

157. Grace Coolidge.

158. What is significant about the Steinway piano in the East Room?

159. Guess the acreage of the White House grounds.

160. Who installed a horseshoe pit on White House grounds?

161. Who called the White House "the great white jail."?

162. Which president got married in the White House?

163. When was Harry Truman told to race through the front and not the side entrance?

164. When was the first telephone hooked up?

165. What was the most prized possession stolen during the British occupation of 1814?

166. When were Easter eggs first rolled on the south lawn?

# ANSWERS

158. In 1938 the Steinway family donated this 300,000th piano bearing their name to the White House.

159. 18.07 acres.

160. George H.W. Bush.

161. President Harry Truman.

162. Grover Cleveland wed Frances Folsom in 1886.

163. When the White House press secretary told him of Franklin Roosevelt's death.

164. 1879.

165. A British lieutenant took President Madison's dress sword.

166. 1879.

167. Which man destroyed nearly all his presidential papers?

168. What happened to almost 100,000 old bricks taken out in the mid 20th century?

169. This president loved to barbecue steaks on the roof.

170. What happened to Lincoln's youngest sons in his first month in office?

171. Which four presidential portraits hung in Richard Nixon's Oval Office?

172. Who held poker games twice a week in the White House?

173. This man was a tailor before getting to the White House.

174. How long did a statue of Thomas Jefferson stand on the front lawn?

175. Who ordered the gilded French chairs now in the Blue Room?

176. How many gallons of paint were used to paint the outside in 1952?

# ANSWERS

167. President Franklin Pierce.

168. Some were sold as souvenirs for $1 each but most were used for rebuilding garden walls and an orangery at Mount Vernon.

169. Dwight Eisenhower.

170. They had measles in the White House.

171. Washington, Theodore Roosevelt, Wilson, and Eisenhower.

172. Warren Harding, with regular members of his "poker cabinet."

173. Andrew Johnson.

174. From 1847 to 1874 when it was returned to the Capitol.

175. James Monroe.

176. 570 gallons.

177. Who refused Abraham Lincoln's invitation to sleep over?

178. How many letters on average arrived daily for President McKinley?

179. This Victorian novelist visited then likened it to an English clubhouse.

180. What were police delegated to do by President Martin Van Buren?

181. What did souvenir hunters take from Zachary Taylor's White House?

182. Who kept a thermometer and a barometer in the entrance hall?

183. Why did President Truman's 92-year-old mother refuse to sleep in the Lincoln bed?

184. How did President Herbert Hoover cut down on handshaking?

185. Who eluded the Secret Service for a four-mile hike?

186. Which first couple boxed slices of their wedding cake for friends?

# ANSWERS

177. Prince Napoleon Bonaparte, the emperor's nephew, who preferred the home of the French Minister.

178. One thousand, which he told his staff to answer within 24 hours.

179. Charles Dickens.

180. Keep out dirty, badly-dressed riff-raff from receptions.

181. Hair plucked from the tail of his grazing war-horse, *Old Whitey*.

182. President Andrew Jackson.

183. A Southern sympathizer, she said she would rather sleep on the floor.

184. He posed for group photos to give his hand a break.

185. Theodore Roosevelt.

186. Grover and Frances Cleveland.

187. When were regular White House press conferences begun?

188. Name the four Presidents who were fathers and sons.

189. For how long after his helicopter left the White House was Richard Nixon still president?

190. Why did the Secret Service trap squirrels?

191. Who was known as *His Accidency* when he entered the White House?

192. How many Americans are estimated to have watched Jackie Kennedy's televised tour of the White House?

193. Which president invited his wife to sit in on cabinet meetings?

194. How many people can be seated in the State Dining Room?

195. How much profit did managing partner George W. Bush make on the sale of the Texas Rangers baseball team?

# ANSWERS

187. To favored newsmen, in Theodore Roosevelt's time, but to the general press in 1913 under Woodrow Wilson.

188. John Adams, John Quincy Adams, George H.W. Bush & George W. Bush.

189. 90 minutes.

190. To remove them from President Eisenhower's putting green.

191. John Tyler, who was the first vice president elevated on the death of an incumbent.

192. About 56 million.

193. Jimmy Carter, though she didn't take part in discussions.

194. 140.

195. Almost $15 million, two years before election to the presidency.

196. When this future president was born his father had been dead 10 weeks.

197. Why was Fala the pet Scottie removed from the East Room during Franklin Roosevelt's funeral service?

198. How long did President Reagan work out in his White House gym?

199. This president poked around the kitchens and even drew up menus.

200. What was the White House called in the earliest years of the Republic?

201. This president entertained his daughters with playful impersonations.

202. How did a King become President?

203. Why did President Jefferson say he would retire after eight years in the White House?

204. How far off could people see the glow from fires set by the British in the White House and Capitol in 1814?

# ANSWERS

196. Rutherford Hayes.

197. Because he was whimpering loudly.

198. About half an hour daily in the late afternoon.

199. Calvin Coolidge.

200. The President's House.

201. Woodrow Wilson.

202. Gerald Ford was born Leslie King, Jr. and renamed for his adoptive father.

203. He gave four reasons: age, inclination, principle, and a yearning for rural life.

204. It was seen from Baltimore, about 45 miles northeast.

205. Reclining on a sofa, this witty president said, "I always talk better when I lie."

206. Why did President Van Buren urge outgoing President Jackson to stay in the White House 3-4 more months?

207. Who wrote that being president was only "dignified slavery."?

208. What did President Arthur return with after resting in Florida from overwork?

209. What did the King of Jordan give Lady Bird Johnson at a State Dinner?

210. What happened when President Coolidge breakfasted with the Senate majority leader?

211. What surprise was in store for President Kennedy had he not been slain?

212. Which president was given the Secret Service code name of Eagle?

213. These men won the White House by defeating 20th century incumbents.

# ANSWERS

205. James Madison.

206. Traveling conditions back to Tennessee would be easier in the spring and summer.

207. Andrew Jackson.

208. Malaria.

209. His menu autographed in Arabic and English.

210. The president told the senator to give his bacon to Coolidge's pet collie.

211. Jackie Kennedy had planned the redecoration of his office.

212. Bill Clinton.

213. Wilson, Franklin Roosevelt, Carter, Reagan, and Clinton.

214. Why were inaugural dates changed from 4 March to 20 January?

215. Which country issued commemorative stamps for Socks, the Clinton's pet cat?

216. Where is the cornerstone, laid with pomp and ceremony in 1792?

217. Why did Theodore Roosevelt refuse to have Christmas trees?

218. Who got a free pail of milk delivered to the White House every morning?

219. Why did President Reagan steer clear of computers and calculators?

220. They had the first color television set in the White House.

221. When was the White House Historical Association formed?

222. The first movie this man saw in the White House was about President Nixon's downfall.

# ANSWERS

214. To shorten the lame-duck period of the presidency.

215. The Central African Republic.

216. Nobody knows exactly where it is.

217. He disapproved of chopping down trees for decorative use.

218. Andrew Jackson, from his close friend, Francis Blair.

219. He said he was too old to learn how to use them.

220. Dwight and Mamie Eisenhower.

221. In 1961.

222. President Carter saw *All the President's Men* two days after moving in.

223. Guess Abraham Lincoln's standard breakfast and lunch.

224. This president was so indifferent to family history that he threw out articles on them.

225. This left-handed president held a tennis racquet in his right hand.

226. When was the north portico added?

227. How long was the White House unoccupied after British arson in 1814?

228. This president called the White House an eight-star hotel.

229. Which president fed a pet mocking bird from his lips?

230. Why did Edith Wilson bar a U.S. Senator from her husband's funeral?

231. Who hired a convicted murderer to look after his young daughter?

# ANSWERS

223. An egg and coffee for breakfast and a biscuit, milk, and fruit for lunch.

224. Grover Cleveland.

225. Gerald Ford.

226. 1830.

227. President James Monroe moved in three years later while rebuilding continued.

228. Ronald Reagan.

229. Thomas Jefferson.

230. Because Senator Henry Cabot Lodge had been President Wilson's severest political foe.

231. President Jimmy Carter.

232. Who suffered from Meniere's Syndrome, an inner-ear disorder causing dizziness and vertigo?

233. Why were Franklin Roosevelt's detailed instructions for his burial not followed?

234. Which Connecticut-born President became Governor of Texas?

235. What work of Italian art is traditionally displayed during Christmas?

236. Which two 20th century presidents probably read the most books?

237. New in the White House, he gave up horseriding for golf.

238. What is the link between the White House and the Purple Heart medal?

239. When did President Grant ban visitors to the White House?

240. When did the White House get its first stables?

241. Why did Helen Taft replace a male steward with a female housekeeper?

# ANSWERS

232. First Lady Mamie Eisenhower.

233. The sealed instructions were delivered to his son after the funeral.

234. George W. Bush, born in New Haven, 6 July 1946.

235. An 18th century creche with 47 carved wood and terra cotta figures.

236. Presidents Theodore Roosevelt and Bill Clinton.

237. President Warren Harding.

238. Pierre L'Enfant designed the medal and selected the site for the White House.

239. On Sundays.

240. 1806.

241. She said no man could recognize details to be supervised.

242. How did Rex, a King Charles spaniel, make it to the White House?

243. When was the Oval Office added?

244. How high was the wedding cake for President Wilson's daughter, Jessie?

245. Whose cabinet members exercised on the south lawn?

246. On which currency note can you see the White House?

247. Whom did British troops toast before setting fire to the White House?

248. What did Abraham Lincoln attach to his luggage as he left home for the White House?

249. How many workmen were photographed in President Taft's bath?

250. Who lies buried on the edge of the Rose Garden?

251. How many visitors walk through the White House annually?

# ANSWERS

242. He was a Christmas gift from Ronald Reagan to his wife, Nancy.

243. 1909.

244. Two feet six inches.

245. President Woodrow Wilson's.

246. A $20 bill.

247. Their Prince Regent and His Majesty's land and naval forces.

248. His own handwritten labels reading A. Lincoln. White House, Washington, D.C.

249. Four.

250. Pete the parakeet, resident during the Eisenhower administration.

251. About one and a half million.

252. A native-born American must be at least this age to be elected president.

253. What did Harry Truman remember to do just after being sworn in on 12 April 1945?

254. What was significant about Ulysses S. Grant living for eight years in the White House?

255. Why did Dolley Madison's drawing room have crimson velvet curtains?

256. Guess the number of chairs in all 23 rooms when Thomas Jefferson left in 1809.

257. How much did the government pay in 1800 for George Washington's portrait in the East Room?

258. What famous tree was slightly damaged by a plane crash in 1994?

259. Which couple celebrated the first Christmas in the White House?

260. Which busts of other presidents did Bill Clinton keep in the Oval Office?

# ANSWERS

252. 35 years old.

253. To phone a pal and cancel their poker game that night.

254. It was the longest time he had lived in one place.

255. Because the decorator could not find silk damask in Philadelphia or New York.

256. 312.

257. $800.

258. The magnolia planted by Andrew Jackson next to the south portico.

259. John and Abigail Adams in 1800.

260. Jefferson, Lincoln, Theodore and Franklin Roosevelt, and Kennedy.

261. Which president hoarded every document that came into his hands?

262. Which first lady said she had only one real hobby, her husband?

263. Who was the first former U.S. Senator elected president?

264. Where did President Madison live after the British burned the White House?

265. Who was the first president to take the oath of office in the White House?

266. When was the basement bomb shelter built?

267. Who was the only president to have a child born in the White House?

268. Which president swam with his glasses on?

269. When did the White House get its first divorced president?

270. What is the name of the most famous White House desk?

# ANSWERS

261. James Buchanan.

262. Florence Harding.

263. James Monroe.

264. In the Octagon, a nearby mansion still standing.

265. Rutherford Hayes.

266. 1951.

267. Grover Cleveland's daughter, Esther, was born 9 September 1893.

268. Harry Truman.

269. In 1981 when Ronald Reagan moved in with second wife Nancy.

270. *Resolute* - made from the oak of a British ship, HMS *Resolute,* and presented to President Hayes by Queen Victoria.

271. A map of Europe in World War 2 hangs over the fireplace in this room.

272. Where did Theodore Roosevelt mount up for his daily horseride?

273. Why was the mansion draped in mourning crepe when President Pierce moved in?

274. Who demanded the White House be built of stone and not brick?

275. This president's father-in-law lived and died in the White House.

276. From how far was water carried into the unfinished White House in 1800?

277. How many times did Mamie Eisenhower enter the Oval Office in eight years?

278. Why did President Coolidge pour cream into a saucer at a State Dinner?

279. What mistake did the Chief Justice make when swearing in Harry Truman?

# ANSWERS

271. The Map Room.

272. On the grounds in front of the south portico.

273. His only surviving son had died in a recent train accident.

274. George Washington.

275. Ulysses S. Grant's father-in-law, Judge Frederick Dent.

276. About five city blocks, from a spring in Franklin Park.

277. Only four times.

278. To feed the cat on the floor.

279. He asked Truman to repeat "I Harry Shippe Truman" when the middle name was a mere initial S.

280. What damage was done by the storm of July 1811?

281. Who brought their favorite velvet-colored furniture to the White House?

282. Which little boy died in the big Lincoln Bed?

283. Warren Harding revived this custom not seen since John Quincy Adams's presidency.

284. How did Andrew Johnson celebrate his 60th birthday?

285. Who called his portrait the ugliest thing he had ever seen?

286. Why was a New Year's Day reception canceled in 1893?

287. When was the first White House wedding of a president's daughter?

288. What happened to Franklin Roosevelt's swimming pool?

# *ANSWERS*

280. Lead flew off the flat roof top.

281. Lady Bird Johnson brought her blue sofa and Richard Nixon his brown easy chair.

282. Willie Lincoln, aged 11.

283. Marine Band concerts on the White House lawns.

284. With a party for several hundred children.

285. Lyndon Johnson.

286. President Benjamin Harrison's granddaughter was sick in the White House with scarlet fever.

287. 1820, when Maria Monroe married her cousin Samuel Gouverneur.

288. It was converted into the Press Room by President Nixon.

289. Who said she wouldn't be proud to invite people in after her first glimpse of the residential quarters?

290. When was the first elevator put in?

291. How did plans for the gardens end up in the Hudson River?

292. What was the original estimated cost of building the White House?

293. How did President Andrew Johnson control New Year's Day crowds?

294. President Chester Arthur kept this day free for himself.

295. Why was water from the Jordan River used in 1889?

296. What did the Prince of Wales send as a thank you for hospitality in 1860?

297. What was the Blue Room called in the 19th century?

298. Why were the number of bodyguards upped from 4 to 27 in 1895?

# ANSWERS

289. First Lady Nancy Reagan.

290. 1882.

291. Landscaper Andrew Jackson Downing drowned when his ship sank in 1852.

292. $400,000.

293. An exit platform led out the East Room window to the northern pavement.

294. Monday, when he refused to see anyone.

295. For the christening of President Benjamin Harrison's granddaughter.

296. A portrait of himself.

297. The Elliptical Saloon.

298. There was a rash of letters threatening President Cleveland.

299. Which president helped subdue a drunken intruder?

300. Why did President McKinley enjoy posing for portrait painters?

301. Why did Abraham Lincoln pause twice before signing the Emancipation Proclamation?

302. Guess the number of pieces of crystal in each East Room chandelier.

303. Which White House bride cut her wedding cake with a sabre?

304. How much did Andrew Jackson pay for his White House piano?

305. This first lady's dying wish was for her devoted husband to remarry.

306. Which president chewed tobacco and if none was available, tore open a cigarette?

307. Malaria struck this first lady within weeks of moving into the White House.

# ANSWERS

299. Benjamin Harrison.

300. He said it was relaxing.

301. His right arm was so stiff after shaking hands for three hours.

302. 6,300.

303. Alice Roosevelt Longworth in 1906.

304. $300 in 1831–but he got back $100 for a trade-in.

305. Ellen Wilson, first wife of Woodrow Wilson, who died in 1914.

306. Warren Harding.

307. Lucretia Garfield.

308. How many windows are in the White House?

309. This president's breakfast always ended with milk.

310. This couple translated a 16th century textbook on mining from Latin into English.

311. Who paid the artist's fee for a death mask of Ulysses S. Grant?

312. Which president loved to recite limericks?

313. How did the Secret Service describe the presidential limousine?

314. Where did Theodore Roosevelt live during expansion and restoration work in 1902?

315. Which 19th century presidents entered the White House as widowers?

316. What caused blisters on the fingers of Abraham Lincoln's right hand?

# ANSWERS

308. 147.

309. Harry Truman.

310. Herbert and Lou Hoover.

311. Mark Twain, after the artist tried to get it from Grant's widow.

312. Woodrow Wilson.

313. Like a tank on four rubber wheels.

314. He moved across the road to 736 Jackson Place on Lafayette Square.

315. Jefferson, Jackson, Van Buren, and Arthur.

316. Thousands of handshakes at a White House reception.

317. Name the only president who was a Campbellite Church member?

318. How long did Woodrow Wilson remain housebound after his 1919 stroke?

319. Whose son harnessed a goat to a chair and drove through a reception?

320. What restrictions were put on the earliest press conferences?

321. What did President Hoover do when he learned of fire in his office?

322. What happened to the dress Rachel Jackson hoped to wear in the White House?

323. When did Richard Nixon tell Gerald Ford he would resign?

324. This president enjoyed painting before turning in at midnight.

325. The Kennedy family donated this painting in memory of John F. Kennedy.

# ANSWERS

317. James Garfield.

318. Five months, then he went for a spin in an auto.

319. Abraham Lincoln's son, Tad.

320. Videotapes were first edited then rebroadcast.

321. He told the Marine Band to continue playing so children partying in the White House would not panic.

322. She was buried in it, only weeks after her husband's electoral victory.

323. At 11 a.m., 9 August 1974.

324. Dwight Eisenhower.

325. Claude Monet's *Morning on the Seine-Fine Weather.*

326. Married twice, this president fathered the most children.

327. What was Franklin Roosevelt doing when he learned of the attack on Pearl Harbor?

328. Which mother-in-law always felt this president wasn't good enough for her daughter?

329. What happened when President Carter phoned President-elect Reagan on inauguration day?

330. Who wrote sarcastically that the White House was a castle well-proportioned to the president's salary?

331. What made Pat Nixon and her daughters flee the family dining room in tears?

332. Why did a Secret Service agent divert President Reagan's car from the White House?

333. A picture of this woman was on Calvin Coolidge's desk when he was governor, vice president and president.

# ANSWERS

326. John Tyler had 15 children.

327. Lunching in his third floor study.

328. Harry Truman's mother-in-law, Madge Wallace.

329. He was told Reagan was sleeping with instructions not to be disturbed.

330. Abigail Adams.

331. A guard accidentally dropped tear gas below an open window.

332. He saw the president coughing blood after an attempted assassination.

333. His mother, Victoria Josephine Coolidge.

QUESTIONS
============

334. Who boosted his own stamp collection
     by saving incoming White House
     stamped envelopes?

335. What was the last thing President
     Wilson did in the White House?

336. How often did President Ford have his
     hair cut?

337. Who had a piece of wood inscribed in
     Latin on his Oval Office desk?

338. Who furnished their private quarters
     with bamboo, palm trees and bird
     cages?

339. What effect did a bullet wound have on
     President Monroe's movement?

340. Why was President George H.W. Bush
     told to keep his distance from his fam-
     ily for a few days?

341. Why did President-elect Taft sleep over
     the night before inauguration?

342. How old was Andrew Jackson when he
     first read the Declaration of
     Independence?

# ANSWERS

334. Franklin Roosevelt.

335. He drank a glass of whisky offered by his doctor.

336. About every 10 days in the White House barber shop.

337. President Eisenhower. It translated *Gently in manner, firmly in deed.*

338. Herbert and Lou Hoover.

339. He appeared to walk with his left side foremost.

340. So they wouldn't become radioactive from the radioactive iodine he was treated with for Graves' disease.

341. President Theodore Roosevelt invited him to quash rumors they had quarreled.

342. He said he was nine years old.

343. Which president walked on the Mall to help find a site for the Smithsonian Institution?

344. Why was President Truman told to move out of his bedroom?

345. What remarkable letters did President Johnson write the night he became president?

346. This couple made a pilgrimage to Thomas Jefferson's home en route to the White House.

347. Who was the youngest man to succeed to the presidency?

348. This first couple decorated their Christmas tree with homemade cookies.

349. Why were 1876 and 1888 unusual in White House history?

350. Who disliked the ritual appearance with a Thanksgiving turkey?

351. Who ordered the swimming pool converted into a press briefing room?

# ANSWERS

343. President James Polk in 1846.

344. The sagging floor was in danger of collapsing.

345. Handwritten letters of comfort to the children of slain President Kennedy.

346. Bill and Hillary Clinton.

347. Theodore Roosevelt was 42 years old.

348. George and Barbara Bush.

349. The office was won by Rutherford Hayes and Benjamin Harrison with fewer popular votes than their opponents.

350. President Ronald Reagan.

351. President Richard Nixon.

352. What did President Eisenhower ask his first day at work?

353. Who pays for White House portraits of presidents and first ladies?

354. Who refused to sell his radio and TV holdings while in office?

355. What was President Grover Cleveland's pet peeve?

356. What surprise was waiting for President Ford after a game of golf?

357. When was the south portico added?

358. How did the wooden floor in the Oval Office floor get nicked?

359. Ronald Reagan had this sign on his Oval Office desk.

360. This man boasted he rose before sunrise for half a century.

361. Who is the only president buried in the Washington Cathedral.

# ANSWERS

352. How to get to the Oval Office.

353. The White House Historical Association, from sales of books, prints, and reproductions of artworks.

354. Lyndon Johnson.

355. Headline-grabbing or politically partisan preachers.

356. His daughter gave him a golden retriever dog she named *Liberty*.

357. 1824.

358. By President Eisenhower's golf cleats.

359. *It Can Be Done.*

360. Thomas Jefferson.

361. Woodrow Wilson.

362. What made President Hoover's hand bleed so badly he had to end a reception?

363. Why was Abraham Lincoln's youngest son, Thomas, nicknamed Tad?

364. Which White House pet is buried next to a president's grave?

365. In which room is the White House Christmas tree displayed?

366. Who decided to be more careful after almost drowning in the Potomac River?

367. How early did President Hoover turn off the lights and go to sleep?

368. Who lost some White House china in a poker bet?

369. Who designated the site for the White House?

370. Who loved to sit in a rocking chair before the fire?

371. What led up to the White House in the early years?

# ANSWERS

362. A guest who shook his hand had a diamond ring turned palmwards.

363. It was short for Tadpole.

364. Fala, the Scottie, next to Franklin Roosevelt at Hyde Park, New York.

365. The Blue Room.

366. John Quincy Adams, who set out on an old boat which sank.

367. 10 p.m.

368. President Warren Harding.

369. Pierre L'Enfant, a French veteran of the Revolutionary War.

370. President Andrew Jackson.

371. Wooden steps.

372. Who said, "You don't live in the White House, you are only exhibit A to the country."?

373. When did suffragettes start picketing the White House?

374. How much of a pay hike did President Taft get?

375. When was a billiard room installed?

376. Name the first White House bride to marry outdoors, in the Rose Garden.

377. What was the Green Room used for in Thomas Jefferson's time?

378. When did the White House get running water and hot and cold showers?

379. Who becomes president if a president-elect dies?

380. Who was the only 20th century president who never went to college?

381. Why did Franklin Roosevelt's coffin remain in the White House only a few hours?

# ANSWERS

372. President Theodore Roosevelt.

373. 1917.

374. Taft got $75,000 and his predecessor Theodore Roosevelt only $50,000.

375. 1970.

376. President Richard Nixon's daughter, Tricia.

377. His dining room.

378. During Andrew Jackson's residency.

379. The 20th Amendment provides for the vice president-elect to become president.

380. Harry Truman.

381. Before his death he said he did not want to lie in state.

382. Who said in 1812 that the president's house leaked like a riddle?

383. About how many letters did Abraham Lincoln receive daily?

384. On what fateful day did President Nixon's wrist watch stop?

385. This man described the presidency as "an easy job."

386. Who was known as "The Dude President"?

387. Lyndon Johnson had this in triplicate in his Oval Office.

388. When was the first telegraph installed?

389. Who was the only president to live in the White House after a four year absence?

390. What happened to the first greenhouse built in 1857?

391. When was a lace curtain stolen?

# ANSWERS

382. The Surveyor of Public Buildings, Benjamin Henry Latrobe.

383. 200–300.

384. At 4 a.m. the day he resigned the presidency.

385. Warren Harding.

386. Chester Arthur, a most fashionably dressed man.

387. Television consoles.

388. In 1866 by Andrew Johnson.

389. Grover Cleveland, elected in 1884 and again in 1892.

390. It was destroyed by fire 10 years later.

391. In 1864, from the East Room.

392. Which two grand rooms are connected by the Cross Hall?

393. How many tons of structural and reinforcing steel were put in during the 1949-52 restorations?

394. How long did Mary Todd Lincoln stay in the White House after her husband's assassination?

395. At what hour did President Chester Arthur breakfast?

396. Which president had the misfortune to shake hands with 8,100 New Year's Day guests?

397. How did the first Japanese diplomats address President Buchanan?

398. Who lobbied successfully for appointment of the first female clerk?

399. Which Russian royal visited the White House in 1871?

400. Why did President McKinley leave the White House on Sundays with a sealed envelope?

# ANSWERS

392. The State Dining Room and the East Room.

393. 910 tons.

394. Five weeks.

395. Between 9 a.m. and 10 a.m.

396. Theodore Roosevelt in 1902.

397. They called him emperor.

398. Edith Wilson persuaded her husband, Woodrow Wilson.

399. The Grand Duke Alexis, son of Czar Alexander.

400. It contained his weekly offering at the Metropolitan Church.

401. How many horses were in Theodore Roosevelt's White House stables?

402. She had a Medal of Honor but Dr. Mary Walker was conspicuous at an 1889 reception for this reason.

403. How did the Women's Christian Temperance Union honor Lucy Hayes for banning liquor?

404. What happened when Queen Victoria's son wanted to dance?

405. Did Andrew Jackson have any regrets the day he left the White House?

406. Who walked four miles then watched the sunrise from a window?

407. Who was the first president to lie in state in the East Room?

408. What did Franklin Roosevelt and George H.W. Bush dislike eating?

409. Whose pay rose from $20,000 to $75,000 a year when he got to the White House?

# ANSWERS

401. Ten - four for carriages and six for the family to ride.

402. As usual, she wore men's clothing.

403. They presented her portrait to the White House.

404. President James Buchanan told him he didn't allow White House dances.

405. Yes - that he didn't hang his vice president, John Calhoun, or shoot Senator Henry Clay.

406. John Quincy Adams.

407. William Henry Harrison in 1841.

408. They both hated broccoli.

409. Vice President Harry Truman.

410. Why were sightseers banned for six years from the White House?

411. Where was Abraham Lincoln's desk discovered before its return to the Hoover White House?

412. What exercise did Richard Nixon do on the morning of his second inaugural?

413. Ladies dresses were torn in the crush to get a better view of this celebrity at the White House.

414. Union troops guarding Abraham Lincoln were quartered in this room.

415. Who died of blood poisoning from a blistered toe after tennis on the south lawn?

416. When was a presidential press conference first televised live?

417. Who benefited from wool sheared off White House sheep?

418. How did all four legs simultaneously break off President Hoover's desk?

# ANSWERS

410. The World War 2 ban continued until 1947.

411. At the Historical Society in Hartford, Connecticut.

412. He ran 500 steps in a fixed position.

413. General Ulysses S. Grant.

414. The East Room.

415. Calvin Coolidge, son of the president.

416. 1961.

417. The Red Cross during World War 1.

418. They broke when his desk was hurriedly moved during a 1929 fire.

# QUESTIONS

419. Who appointed the first White House physician?

420. In which room did President Nixon televise his resignation speech?

421. When did Congress restore General Eisenhower's five-star rank?

422. What did Jackie Kennedy find in a White House men's room?

423. Where did Andrew Johnson's cabinet meet while Lincoln's widow prepared to leave?

424. How did Franklin Roosevelt bypass his housekeeper's awful food?

425. Why did Congressmen call John Adams *His Rotundity?*

426. Why did President Truman cross the front lawn on 14 August 1945?

427. What helped get mobs out of the White House after Andrew Jackson's inauguration?

# ANSWERS

419. William McKinley.

420. The Oval Office.

421. In 1961, the year he left the White House.

422. Long lost marble busts of George Washington, Martin Van Buren, and Christopher Columbus.

423. In the adjacent Treasury building.

424. He ate meals from a separate kitchen next to his study.

425. Because he wanted high-sounding titles for political leaders.

426. To greet jubilant throngs after Japan's surrender in World War 2.

427. Whisky dispensed on the lawn.

# QUESTIONS

428. Who appointed the first female White House physician?

429. Why does the Secret Service not help the President carry anything?

430. Who died at his White House desk?

431. What tune came out of a cigar case on President Nixon's desk?

432. Why do most presidents dislike official motorcades?

433. Why was the wife of the French President unable to move in the State Dining Room?

434. These presidents would not let bands play *Hail to the Chief* in their presence.

435. Which president went to sleep after being sworn in?

436. What did President Wilson read the night before the end of World War 1?

437. Republican Gerald Ford kept a bust of this Democrat in his office.

# ANSWERS

428. President Kennedy named Dr. Janet Travell in 1961.

429. Their hands must be free at all times to defend the president.

430. Charlie Ross, press secretary to President Truman.

431. *Hail to the Chief.*

432. The inconvenience to motorists and an impression of superiority.

433. President Reagan was standing on the hem of her gown.

434. Grover Cleveland and William Howard Taft.

435. Calvin Coolidge was sworn in at 2.47 a.m. then turned out the lights at 3 a.m.

436. A chapter of the Bible.

437. Harry Truman.

438. How did President Jefferson regularly exercise?

439. For whom was the swimming pool heated to 87 degrees?

440. Why did President Eisenhower pound his blankets with his fists?

441. What did newly-inaugurated President Taft do when addressed as *Mr. President?*

442. This president threatened to punch the nose of a music critic.

443. Who longed to be near his wife's tomb to lie down beside her?

444. Who returned to the White House as guest of honor 32 years after leaving as first lady?

445. What made President Polk scurry to Bedford Springs, Pennsylvania in 1848?

446. Why did Lyndon Johnson wake his wife at 4:20 a.m. on 5 June 1968?

# ANSWERS

438. He went horseback riding between 1 and 3 p.m.

439. President Kennedy, suffering from back pains.

440. He was frustrated by loss of memory and difficulty in speaking after a stroke.

441. He turned to see whether his predecessor was standing beside him.

442. President Truman, after the critic savaged daughter Margaret Truman's singing abilities.

443. Andrew Jackson.

444. Dolley Madison.

445. He was worn out from work and had not been more than three miles from the White House in 13 months.

446. To see the TV bulletins on Bobby Kennedy's assassination.

447. What is fixed to the fireplace in the bedroom where Presidents Lincoln and Kennedy slept?

448. Bananas and peanut butter were a delicacy for this president.

449. At what hour and on what day does the White House normally get a new occupant?

450. How did bullets strike the White House in 1994?

451. Two days before leaving the White House this man wrote he felt more relief than a prisoner released from chains.

452. What was conspicuous on the Eisenhower's family Christmas tree?

453. This first lady consulted an astrologer to coordinate the president's schedule.

454. Why was President Truman often resident without his wife?

# ANSWERS

447. Commemorative plaques giving the dates of their occupancies.

448. Bill Clinton.

449. Barring election or death, the 20th Amendment says a president's term ends at noon on 20 January.

450. A man fired a rifle from Pennsylvania Avenue before being arrested.

451. President Thomas Jefferson.

452. Glass ornaments with rocket designs, the gift of Soviet leader Nikita Khrushchev.

453. Nancy Reagan.

454. Bess Truman hated the limelight of Washington and often returned home to Independence, Missouri.

455. Why did the President's Foreign Intelligence Advisory Board abandon lunch in the mess?

456. This first couple went up to the roof with a telescope to look at stars and planets.

457. What was President Ford's Sunday morning delight?

458. What did Grover Cleveland do with White House memorabilia when his Manhattan lease expired?

459. How did George Washington change the winning design for the White House?

460. How did James Monroe's diplomatic stay in France influence his White House residency?

461. Which president described the White House as a goldfish bowl.

462. How did Franklin Roosevelt's radio talks become known as fireside chats?

463. Who allowed himself only one egg a week in the White House?

# *ANSWERS*

455. News arrived of President Kennedy's assassination.

456. Jimmy and Rosalynn Carter.

457. Waffles with sour cream, strawberries, and maple syrup.

458. He threw away most of it, especially handwritten documents.

459. He enlarged the width and length by 20 per cent.

460. He and his wife Elizabeth spoke French and brought in French furniture.

461. Harry Truman.

462. His press secretary said Roosevelt imagined chatting with a few people around his fireside.

463. President Ronald Reagan.

464. What made President Jefferson take to French cuisine?

465. What did Woodrow Wilson have at home to remind him of chiming White House clocks?

466. Who refused at first to have a telephone in his office?

467. This president exercised by throwing a medicine ball over a net.

468. How did Franklin Roosevelt's grand-children haunt an overnight guest?

469. Why did President Harding's wife keep him away from the White House one Christmas?

470. Who died a pauper almost four decades after deciding where to build the White House?

471. When was a rail fence surrounding the White House taken away?

472. Who hired a Swedish cook for the White House?

# ANSWERS

464. He said it made meat more tender.

465. A grandfather clock that chimed every quarter hour.

466. Calvin Coolidge, who went into another room for important calls.

467. Herbert Hoover.

468. They draped a sheet over clothes stuffed with paper and left it outside the guest's bedroom.

469. They stayed with friends after an anonymous letter threatened assassination on Christmas.

470. Pierre L'Enfant's possessions were worth $45 at his death in 1825.

471. 1807.

472. First Lady Helen Taft.

473. When was the first tennis court built?

474. How many fireplaces are in the White House?

475. This first lady's portrait features her white collie, Rob Roy.

476. Which president was later elected to the House of Representatives?

477. Which band has performed at every inauguration since 1801?

478. Which occupant chose the first books for the White House library?

479. What did President Nixon order for his last White House breakfast?

480. This president invited the public to come in and shake hands daily between 12.30 p.m. and lunch.

481. How many gallons of paint were used inside 1949-52?

482. How did President McKinley cut down on White House visitors?

# ANSWERS

473. 1902.

474. 29.

475. Grace Coolidge.

476. John Quincy Adams.

477. The U.S. Marine Band.

478. Abigail Fillmore.

479. His favorite of corned beef hash and poached eggs.

480. Warren Harding.

481. 895 gallons.

482. Invitation cards were no longer seasonal but restricted to a single reception.

483. How old is the East Room oak floor?

484. Why did President Franklin Pierce install the first furnace in the White House?

485. Where did President Hoover work after his office wing was damaged by fire?

486. Why was a bilingual secretary added to Jackie Kennedy's staff?

487. What made Herbert Hoover cry in Harry Truman's Oval Office?

488. What gaffe was committed during the 1978 arrival of the Roumanian president?

489. When did former President Nixon drop his Secret Service protection?

490. Who appointed the first female aide to carry the bag with nuclear codes?

491. What flashed through Calvin Coolidge's mind on learning he had succeeded to the presidency?

# ANSWERS

483. It dates back to 1902.

484. His doctors attributed his coughing to the cold and damp White House.

485. He moved into the State, War, and Navy building next door.

486. She received so much mail from French-speaking fans.

487. He was so touched by Truman's invitation to head up food relief to Europe.

488. Roumania had a new anthem but the band played the old tune.

489. Eleven years after leaving the White House.

490. President Ronald Reagan.

491. He said he believed he could "swing it."

492. Who gave only two public speeches during eight years in the White House?

493. This president was a bachelor until age 35.

494. Which president had migraine headaches for 10 days at a time?

495. Why were Eleanor Roosevelt's dogs banished to Hyde Park, New York?

496. Why did former President Theodore Roosevelt refuse to visit the White House?

497. Who smoked heavily when irritated?

498. What was President Andrew Jackson's favorite pipe?

499. Why did President Woodrow Wilson like the number 13?

500. Why did Thomas Jefferson believe two elected terms were the most a president should serve?

501. How long did Gilbert Stuart take to finish the portrait of First Lady Louisa Adams?

# *ANSWERS*

492. Thomas Jefferson.

493. President Gerald Ford.

494. Thomas Jefferson.

495. For biting a U.S. Senator and a journalist.

496. He didn't think it a good idea for ex-presidents to go to Washington, except when they couldn't help it.

497. Jackie Kennedy.

498. A corn cob which he called "the sweetest and best pipe."

499. There were 13 letters in his name and there were 13 original colonies.

500. Otherwise supporters might keep him in power long after he had become old and doddering.

501. Five years.

502. What news made hospitalized Lyndon Johnson's temperature rise?

503. Who outshone the president at a White House reception on New Year's Day 1825?

504. This first lady was formerly counsel on the House Judiciary Committee considering impeachment of President Nixon.

505. If he had not taken the name of his stepfather he would have been President Blythe.

506. *The Reader's Digest* was one of the favorite magazines of this president.

507. When were White House correspondents allowed to quote the president directly?

508. Senior White House staff stood in her bedroom while she sat in bed giving daily instructions.

509. How did a first lady become president?

510. When was the only unelected vice president sworn in as president?

# ANSWERS

502. The announcement of Winston Churchill's death.

503. Hero of the Revolutionary War, the Marquis de Lafayette, then visiting Washington.

504. Hillary Rodham Clinton.

505. Bill Clinton, whose biological father, William Blythe, died three months before his son's birth.

506. President Ronald Reagan.

507. During the Eisenhower administration.

508. Mamie Eisenhower.

509. Caroline Harrison was president general of the Daughters of the American Revolution.

510. Gerald Ford, on 9 August 1974.

# NRSA

WHITE/TORIE

SEAT

BIRMINGHAM
ATLANTA

DL1506                    02MAY

Operated By:
DELTA AIR LINES, INC

511. Every Thursday this president lunched with his vice president.

512. Which president piggy-backed a man over a stream then left without revealing his identity?

513. Shortly before his death this president dreamed he saw his corpse in the White House.

514. How did John Quincy Adams treat Congressmen who frequented "gin lane and beer alley"?

515. Who suffered from chronic indigestion?

516. Who loved the sports pages, particularly boxing news?

517. When was a carriage house built for the White House?

518. When were the grounds reopened to the public after closure in World War 1?

519. Who placed footmen in blue livery at the front entrance?

# *ANSWERS*

511. President Reagan lunched with Vice President George Bush.

512. Thomas Jefferson.

513. Abraham Lincoln.

514. He said they had lost their right to polite treatment.

515. Andrew Jackson.

516. President Warren Harding.

517. 1809.

518. 1921.

519. First Lady Helen Taft, to be conspicuous to answer visitors' questions.

520. Which president thought the Psalms were the best poetry ever written?

521. Which room did the Nixons use as a family room?

522. What movie did Franklin Roosevelt screen for Prime Minister Winston Churchill?

523. Harry Truman walked a lot. What was his shoe size?

524. This first lady spoke five languages including Chinese.

525. Why was wounded Abraham Lincoln not taken back to the White House?

526. Who often wheeled his chair to view the spire of St. John's Church across the road?

527. What did Harry Truman give President Kennedy at the latter's inaugural lunch?

528. Who described her family as "plain people called here for a short time by a calamity."

# ANSWERS

520. John Adams.

521. The third floor solarium.

522. *The Battle of Britain.*

523. 9B.

524. Lou Hoover.

525. Doctors decided to place him on the nearest available bed.

526. President William McKinley.

527. An autographed copy of the menu.

528. Martha Patterson, daughter of newly-installed President Andrew Johnson.

529. What delayed Harry Truman's swearing in at the White House in 1945?

530. Who slept in the Lincoln Bed on President Carter's first night in office?

531. Over which state was Richard Nixon's plane when he ceased to be president?

532. How was Ronald Reagan dressed when President Carter phoned to concede defeat in 1980?

533. How much did Calvin Coolidge contract for his memoirs?

534. How did John Adams describe the White House in 1800?

535. A voracious reader of books, this president hardly read newspapers.

536. The desk of this president had a metal football with a plate inscribed *South High Football Club.*

537. Why did President Jefferson ride without an escort to his successor's inauguration?

# ANSWERS

529. It took time to find a Bible.

530. Rosalynn Carter's mother.

531. Missouri.

532. He was taking a shower.

533. $5 a word.

534. "The building is in a state to be habitable."

535. Theodore Roosevelt.

536. Gerald Ford.

537. He left the White House only with a grandson to avoid ostentation.

538. Who gave the first press conference by a first lady?

539. Which president ignored protocol by always sitting next to his wife at official dinners?

540. Where did Andrew Jackson escape assassination when a pistol jammed?

541. Where did President Polk, a Methodist, and his wife Sarah, a Presbyterian, regularly worship?

542. What did President Lyndon Johnson love to eat?

543. What did John F. Kennedy's staff give him on his last birthday?

544. Which president had a foreign capital named after him?

545. Whose approval rating plunged from 91 per cent the year before his ouster from the White House?

546. With President Reagan wounded by an assassin, what were the secretaries of state and defense arguing over?

# *ANSWERS*

538. Eleanor Roosevelt.

539. William McKinley.

540. In the U.S. Capitol after funeral services for a Congressman.

541. At the First Presbyterian Church.

542. Hash with jalapenos.

543. A surprise party and boxing gloves to take on Congress.

544. Monrovia, capital of Liberia, is named in honor of James Monroe.

545. President George H.W. Bush.

546. They both claimed command.

547. Which first lady tried to scrub clean a carpet soiled by her dog?

548. On what exact date did James Hoban win the design for the White House?

549. Who had a sign on his desk reading *The Buck Stops Here?*

550. How heavy was the cheese given to President Jefferson by foreign-born citizens in Pennsylvania?

551. What happened when the Lone Ranger asked that donations of dimes for a polio foundation be sent to the White House?

552. Where did Lady Bird Johnson start writing her memoirs?

553. In which room did President Nixon sign his letter of resignation?

554. What historic event took place on President Truman's 61st birthday?

555. Was the first live presidential press conference held in the White House?

# ANSWERS

547. Mamie Eisenhower.

548. 17 July 1792.

549. President Harry Truman.

550. 1235 lbs.

551. So many arrived they were sent to the Treasury in armored cars.

552. In her northwest Washington home two weeks before moving into the White House.

553. The second floor Lincoln Sitting Room, normally his night study.

554. On 8 May 1945 the Germans surrendered in World War 2.

555. No, it was in the State Department auditorium.

556. Why did concert pianist Vladimir Horowitz refuse to play at the White House?

557. What made First Lady Pat Nixon pine for Camp David?

558. What did President Reagan regularly eat for lunch?

559. How did Calvin "Silent Cal" Coolidge reply to those who made fun of his silences?

560. How did partially paralyzed Woodrow Wilson describe his walking cane?

561. How did President Ford, adopted in infancy, first meet his biological father?

562. This president cut public receptions to the Fourth of July and New Year's Day.

563. How long after a bullet lodged in Andrew Jackson's shoulder did he have it removed?

564. Guess who said that there was no leisure time for a conscientious president.

# ANSWERS

556. He waited for the 50th anniversary of his first U.S. performance then accepted another invitation to the White House.

557. Away from the White House, she could exercise, particularly walk and swim.

558. Soup and fruit.

559. He said he could have a better time listening than talking.

560. He called it his third leg.

561. He was in high school working a hamburger stand when his father came in and introduced himself.

562. Thomas Jefferson.

563. Nineteen years after it was fired in 1813.

564. President James Polk.

565. How many viewers watched President Truman's televised tour of the White House?

566. *History Today* was one of the favorite magazines of this president.

567. Who left the White House on Thanksgiving to carve a turkey for the homeless?

568. Which president retired to a state where his son was governor?

569. His study had books, carpenter's tools, paint, scientific instruments, maps, and gardening tools.

570. Why did the 1973 Christmas tree have 80 per cent fewer lights?

571. How many years was Franklin Roosevelt afflicted with polio?

572. This piano-playing president was fond of Chopin's music.

573. How old was George H.W. Bush when he became the youngest Navy pilot?

# ANSWERS

565. Thirty million.

566. John F. Kennedy.

567. President Bill Clinton.

568. George Bush, who retired in Texas.

569. Thomas Jefferson.

570. Electricity savings following the Arab oil embargo after war in the Mideast.

571. From 1921 until his death 24 years later.

572. Harry Truman.

573. 18 in 1943.

574. Why didn't George Washington live in the White House?

575. Which first couple regularly ate dinner off trays while watching TV?

576. John Hinckley Jr. stalked this man before shooting President Reagan.

577. Why did Calvin Coolidge's father swear him into office?

578. Guess how many times a day President Ford filled his pipe with tobacco?

579. What was distinctive about President Jefferson as he rode the streets of Washington?

580. How did the King of Jordan find a dance partner when barred by protocol from making the first move?

581. This man threatened to "thrash" reporters who wrote false stories about his family.

582. What happened to a man who punched President Jackson in the face?

# ANSWERS

574. His presidency ended in 1797, he died in 1799, and the White House was ready for occupation only in 1800.

575. Ronald and Nancy Reagan.

576. President Jimmy Carter.

577. He was a notary public and both were in the father's home when word came of President Harding's death.

578. Eight.

579. He usually wore his hat almost down to eye level.

580. A female White House correspondent asked him for a dance.

581. President Woodrow Wilson at a 1914 press conference.

582. He fled, but Jackson said he would have killed him if he had caught him.

583. What happened to a Congressman who went to the White House to borrow $100 from President Polk?

584. What did Lyndon Johnson invariably do when ill?

585. This couple laughed at each other in disbelief the morning after his election.

586. Which couple started the tradition of having the presidential bedrooms in the southwest corner?

587. Where did the White House stones come from?

588. When is the grand staircase used?

589. How old are the twin chandeliers in the Cross Hall?

590. Who decided to display the White House china collection?

591. Whose kids roller-skated in the East Room?

# ANSWERS

583. He got the loan from his old friend but committed suicide two days later.

584. Sweat through two or three pairs of pajamas.

585. Bill and Hillary Clinton.

586. John and Abigail Adams.

587. Aquia Creek quarry in Virginia.

588. When the president and his guest of honor descend for State Dinners.

589. They were made at the end of the 18th century in England.

590. First Lady Edith Wilson.

591. President Theodore Roosevelt's.

592. When were marble busts of Columbus and Vespucci spray painted by a vandal?

593. Where was the gilded wood chandelier in the Red Room made?

594. When was the State Dining Room given its name?

595. Where did Chester Arthur live while the White House was redecorated?

596. Who died five days after gorging on cherries and iced milk?

597. Who played matchmaker for President Van Buren's son Abraham and the beautiful Angelica Singleton?

598. What happened the first time gas lights lit up a reception?

599. How many fireplaces were lit to keep the new building warm and dry?

600. Did President Wilson marry his second wife in the White House?

# ANSWERS

592. In 1998 by a woman who was arrested by the Secret Service.

593. In France in 1805.

594. During Andrew Jackson's tenure.

595. In the home of a U.S. Senator on Capitol Hill.

596. President Zachary Taylor in 1850.

597. Former First Lady Dolley Madison.

598. They failed and candles were lit.

599. Thirteen.

600. No. They wed at her house on 20th Street in northwest Washington.

601. During whose administration was the White House infested with cockroaches?

602. When he got to the White House he was the first former governor and legislator in both state houses.

603. Who opened a kindergarten school on the top floor?

604. Who read aloud to his wife while she painted chinaware?

605. Why did Woodrow Wilson wake up in the middle of the night?

606. What did President Polk do when a fanatical Presbyterian objected to appointment of Catholics as army chaplains?

607. What happened when a housekeeper criticized a fish dish for a State Dinner?

608. In whose White House was water said to flow like wine?

609. Why did President Carter nap instead of sleep for three solid days?

# ANSWERS

601. Grover Cleveland's.

602. Andrew Johnson.

603. Jackie Kennedy, for daughter Caroline.

604. Benjamin Harrison.

605. To comfort his dying first wife, Ellen.

606. He cited the constitutional separation of church and state.

607. The enraged cook destroyed a platter with boiling hot water.

608. Rutherford and Lucy Hayes, who banned liquor and wine.

609. He had to follow negotiations for release of the U.S. hostages in Iran.

610. Who refused to continue the tradition of giving White House clerks Christmas gifts?

611. Who did Franklin Roosevelt insist had to be in the White House for his final inauguration?

612. What was Abraham Lincoln invisibly infected with when he delivered the Gettysburg Address?

613. What used to face the White House before it was built?

614. A picture by this former president hung in President Reagan's hospital room.

615. What non-vegetarian dishes were served at a State Dinner for the Indian premier?

616. Where was President Madison when the British burned the White House?

617. A reporter said this president stood like a soldier on parade, chin in, chest out.

618. How did President Polk react when a drunken son of a U.S. Senator left shouting profanities?

# ANSWERS

610. President William Howard Taft.

611. All 13 of his grandchildren.

612. He had the first invisible signs of small-pox.

613. A farm house with apple orchard.

614. A watercolor of a horse and wagon by Ulysses S. Grant.

615. Seafood and pheasant.

616. He fled to Virginia.

617. Theodore Roosevelt.

618. Shocked, he called him ill-mannered, impertinent, and worthless.

619. Who built a swimming pool just south of the Oval Office?

620. In which suite did Prime Minister Winston Churchill sleep in 1941?

621. Why did the widow Florence Harding prevent her famous Airedale dog from breeding?

622. What did Franklin Roosevelt continue to drink after the repeal of Prohibition?

623. Which president was disgusted by "loafers" who asked him for military commissions?

624. What was Franklin Roosevelt's nickname for his bossy housekeeper?

625. Supreme Court Justices wrote to this dying man praising his "golden heart."

626. Why did President Johnson give a red, white and blue Victorian mailbox to the Japanese premier?

627. What was Franklin Roosevelt's blood pressure the year America went to war?

# ANSWERS

619. President Gerald Ford.

620. In the Rose Suite on the second floor.

621. She wanted his line to die with him.

622. Home brewed beer.

623. James Polk.

624. *Fluffy.*

625. Chief Justice and former President William Howard Taft.

626. The premier was a former postmaster general of Japan.

627. 188 over 105.

# QUESTIONS

628. Which first lady joked she would feed reporters to her puppy?

629. When did White House plasterers strike?

630. Why did Harry Truman live across the road for most of his second term?

631. Why did Franklin Roosevelt tell a cabinet member to come over with a violin?

632. Why did armed guards deliver a 92 lb. pie to President Taft?

633. Who are always on the White House roof?

634. Where do the white marble mantels come from in the Green Room?

635. This man was the first Catholic elected to the White House.

636. Why was the chandelier removed from the Blue Room in 1970?

637. How did James Madison begin wooing the widow Dolley Payne Todd?

# ANSWERS

628. Jackie Kennedy.

629. 1951.

630. The decaying White House was gutted and reinforced with steel and concrete.

631. To play it during a break in a late night marathon work session.

632. Because a thief earlier made off with a 50 lb. pie sent for Thanksgiving.

633. Security specialists.

634. Carrara, Italy.

635. John F. Kennedy.

636. To accommodate the 19 foot-high Christmas tree.

637. While boarding in her father's house he gave her a book.

638. How did 19th century wallpaper from a Maryland house end up on the Diplomatic Reception Room?

639. This first lady did not like her Secret Service code name of Victoria.

640. Who put up the controversial balcony in the south portico?

641. For weekend relief from heat, this president built log cabins 100 miles away in Virginia.

642. What happened when the cook told Lou Hoover she had voted for her husband's opponent?

643. What happened when President Clinton introduced his new dog to his old cat?

644. What was the first public event in the rebuilt White House after the fire of 1814?

645. What made Lyndon Johnson leave the White House for late-night visits to a Benedictine church?

# ANSWERS

638. An individual bought the wallpaper before the house was destroyed and showed it to Jackie Kennedy.

639. Lady Bird Johnson.

640. President Truman in 1947.

641. Herbert Hoover.

642. Mrs. Hoover said she was interested only in her cooking, not her politics.

643. Barking and hissing, they had to be held apart.

644. A presidential reception on New Year's Day 1818.

645. He found solace there during some of the worst moments of the Vietnam War.

646. Why were the first U.S. Senators opposed to the title *President of the United States?*

647. The son of this president won the Congressional Medal of Honor.

648. Where did Woodrow Wilson look as he drove past the White House after his successor was sworn in?

649. What did President Taft admit was his life's ambition?

650. Jimmy Carter admired this former president more than any other.

651. A visitor said this president looked like a schoolmaster in mourning for whipping a pupil to death.

652. This future president won a trip to Washington and shook hands with President Kennedy.

653. Which first lady let her daughter become White House hostess.

# *ANSWERS*

646. It was too common: there were already presidents of fire companies and cricket clubs.

647. Webb Hayes, son of Rutherford and Lucy Hayes, for uncommon valor in the Philippines.

648. Away from the White House, towards Lafayette Square.

649. To be Chief Justice of the United States, which he became in 1921.

650. Harry Truman.

651. James Madison.

652. Sixteen-year-old high school student, Bill Clinton.

653. Eliza Johnson.

654. Which first lady sat by her husband's coffin in the East Room and said no one could now hurt him?

655. What did President Tyler refer to as his "candle-box on wheels?"

656. These three former White House occupants died on Fourth of July.

657. Which of the early presidents began summering at the Soldiers' Home in Maryland?

658. He graduated from college at 17 and got to the White House 34 years later.

659. Why did James Monroe stay in the same clothes for 10 days and nights?

660. Who was first to go through the receiving line at Tricia Nixon's wedding?

661. What made President-elect Jefferson furious with President Adams?

662. Why did former President Taft say he could not practice law as an advocate?

# ANSWERS

654. Florence Harding.

655. His one-horse carriage.

656. John Adams, Thomas Jefferson, and James Monroe.

657. James Buchanan in 1857.

658. John Tyler.

659. He said he was too busy as secretary of state and acting secretary of war before and after the British occupation of Washington, D.C.

660. Former First Lady Mamie Eisenhower.

661. Adams appointed a chief justice on the eve of Jefferson's presidency.

662. Because he had appointed six of the nine Supreme Court Justices and 45 per cent of the federal judiciary.

663. Who advised his teenage daughter to "be friendly with all and too friendly with none."

664. Where did President Clinton place a bust of Abraham Lincoln?

665. Who would have moved in if President Nixon had died immediately after Vice President Agnew's resignation?

666. Who was said to dine very simply on bread, milk, and vegetables?

667. Unlike his modern predecessors, this incumbent never owned a home.

668. What did Eleanor Roosevelt give Fala, the pet Scottie, for Christmas?

669. This president said he was poorer when he left the White House after eight years.

670. Who sometimes ordered the lawns sprayed with green paint to hide patches?

671. This president gave his vice-president more visibility than any previous number two.

# ANSWERS

663. Andrew Johnson.

664. On a table just behind his Oval Office desk.

665. Speaker of the House of Representatives Carl Albert, until two days later when Gerald Ford was appointed vice president.

666. Andrew Jackson.

667. President Clinton.

668. A stocking stuffed with rubber bones.

669. Andrew Jackson.

670. Jackie Kennedy.

671. President Bill Clinton and Vice President Al Gore.

672. Who rode to work at the White House twice a week from his rented country home in the summer.

673. A stickler for protocol, this first lady refused to admit an inappropriately dressed relative.

674. What was it about President Taft that was described as "a national possession."

675. What happened when civic leaders told President Jefferson they wanted to celebrate his birthday?

676. When did White House guards abandon their posts?

677. Whose baby granddaughter died in the White House in 1840?

678. What did President Harding describe as the most distressful decision of his life?

679. Why did a doctor inject brandy into the arm of Ulysses S. Grant?

680. Who possessed George Healy's portrait of Abraham Lincoln before it ended up in the White House?

# ANSWERS

672. President Martin Van Buren.

673. Elizabeth Monroe.

674. His chuckle.

675. He told them the only birthday he commemorated was that of America's independence.

676. Just before the British captured Washington in August 1814.

677. President Martin Van Buren's, his first grandchild.

678. Selling his newspaper, the Marion, Ohio *Star*, shortly before his death.

679. To revive him and relieve the pain from throat cancer.

680. Lincoln's granddaughter, Mary Lincoln Isham, had it bequeathed to her for life by her mother, after which it was to be public property.

681. This president often dined with guests under a magnolia tree.

682. How did Abigail Adams walk through closed doors in the White House?

683. When did staff call the White House the Malacanan Palace?

684. Who donated the 18th century French musical clock in the Red Room?

685. What did Pat Nixon dislike about her White House portrait?

686. Thomas Jefferson said if this president's soul was turned inside out it would be found spotless.

687. When was the oldest surviving glassware acquired?

688. Who revealed the secret taping system in the Nixon White House?

689. Who organized White House pool bets for major sports events?

# ANSWERS

681. Herbert Hoover.

682. White House legend says her ghost has been seen doing this.

683. When President Taft, a former Governor of the Philippines, brought in oriental furniture.

684. French President Vincent Auriol in 1952.

685. She said her mouth made her look sad.

686. James Monroe.

687. 1829 from a Pittsburgh firm.

688. Alexander Butterworth.

689. Franklin Roosevelt.

690. Which White House occupant thought he was dying during two hours of incapacitating cramps and convulsions?

691. What was the last function attended by John F. Kennedy at the White House?

692. Which outgoing president helped his successor receive White House guests?

693. Who built a White House grapery?

694. Who refused to allow aides to forge his autograph when so many requests came for signed photos?

695. Who invited White House staff to parties at their farm?

696. Who chose his boyhood friend to be White House press secretary?

697. What will be opened on 13 October 2092?

698. Who inaugurated the exclusive White House Fellows program to train future U.S. leaders in government operations?

# ANSWERS

690. President James Monroe.

691. An evening Judiciary Reception.

692. Millard Fillmore assisted President Franklin Pierce.

693. President Ulysses S. Grant.

694. Franklin Roosevelt.

695. Dwight and Mamie Eisenhower.

696. Harry Truman appointed Pulitzer prizewinner Charlie Ross.

697. The time capsule buried with a letter from President Bush and a copy of *Millie's Book* by Barbara Bush.

698. President Lyndon Johnson.

699. Where did Eleanor Roosevelt stable the horse she rode in Rock Creek Park?

700. Who said she wanted to make the White House "the first house in the land."

701. Who had a reputation for wearing trousers that were too short?

702. Which president was the first to invite his doctor to live in the White House?

703. Who was the first President to benefit from an annual salary doubled to $400,000 per year?

704. How long had John F. Kennedy been married when he was killed?

705. What happened to Bob the pet canary when the widow Florence Harding left the White House?

706. In which rooms have most sightings been made of ghosts?

707. Which president astonished the staff when he ordered toothpicks placed on the table?

# ANSWERS

699. Across the Potomac River at Fort Myer, Virginia.

700. Jackie Kennedy, shortly before directing redecorations.

701. Abraham Lincoln.

702. James Buchanan.

703. George W. Bush.

704. Ten years.

705. She gave him to a member of the household staff.

706. The Lincoln Bedroom, the Rose Room and the northwest corner room.

707. Warren Harding.

708. This president said his face looked like he was a cold and canny Scot.

709. What does every president refrain from doing at Ford's Theater in downtown Washington?

710. What was President Kennedy allergic to?

711. Which first lady was a heat freak, often complaining that the White House was too cold?

712. Which remarkable cellist performed in the White House in 1904 and again in 1961?

713. To which country could President Martin Van Buren trace his ancestry?

714. What did the staff nickname President Herbert Hoover?

715. Why did President Coolidge receive aviator Charles Lindbergh in a rented mansion instead of the White House?

716. Which man entered the White House with a Pulitzer Prize for a book?

# ANSWERS

708. Woodrow Wilson.

709. No president ever sits in the box where Abraham Lincoln was sitting when he was assassinated.

710. The hair on cats and dogs.

711. Nancy Reagan.

712. Pablo Casals.

713. Holland.

714. His Majesty.

715. He was staying at a downtown mansion while the White House roof was strengthened.

716. John F. Kennedy for *Profiles in Courage*.

717. What was special about the Phaeton conveying Martin Van Buren to his inauguration?

718. Who were White House residents Leon and Diana?

719. What name did the Secret Service give John F. Kennedy?

720. Where does the general public enter the White House for tours?

721. Why did Nellie Grant have orange blossoms in her hair?

722. Why are the names of all cabinet members on brass plaques in the White House?

723. Which first lady had her hometown bridge club visit for several days?

724. After leaving the White House this widower married his wife's niece.

725. At what sad moment did visitors steal some White House keepsakes?

# ANSWERS

717. It was made from the original oak of the frigate Constitution.

718. Cuban blood-hounds given to Andrew Jackson.

719. Lancer.

720. Through the gate to the East Wing on East Executive Boulevard.

721. For her bridal appearance at the White House wedding in 1874.

722. The plaques are fixed to their individual chairs around the cabinet table.

723. Bess Truman.

724. President Benjamin Harrison.

725. When the White House was open to public mourners following the assassination of Abraham Lincoln.

726. On what floor is the Vermeil Room with the display of gilded silver?

727. What did President Thomas Jefferson build around the south grounds?

728. Where did Millie the spaniel give birth to six pups?

729. When was the original White House architect, James Hoban, honored with a 20c postage stamp?

730. How did the closely-knit Truman family start the day together?

731. Which first lady put an end to giving away chipped and cracked White House china?

732. Why was a stairway which had been in place more than a quarter century removed in 1902?

733. Who wrote "I will return" on slips of paper and tucked them under carpets and behind paintings?

734. Who decorated the East Room with false beams and Corinthian columns?

# ANSWERS

726. The ground floor.

727. A wall.

728. In First Lady Barbara Bush's beauty parlor on the second floor.

729. In 1981.

730. They breakfasted together.

731. Edith Roosevelt.

732. To enlarge the State Dining Room.

733. President Eisenhower's young grandson, David.

734. President Ulysses S. Grant.

735. Which president had a quotation of Mark Twain framed on his desk?

736. Who installed a bowling alley in the White House?

737. Whose portraits frame the mantel in the Blue Room?

738. Who said the Lincoln Bed looked like a cathedral?

739. When was the first refrigerator brought into the White House?

740. Why was the Roosevelt Room known as "the morgue" when Franklin Roosevelt was president?

741. When were scorch marks found on some of the stones from fires dating back to British arson in 1814?

742. In which room is the portrait of Dolley Madison by Gilbert Stuart?

743. How many heads of state did the Eisenhowers entertain when they broke the record of all previous occupants?

# ANSWERS

735. Harry Truman. It read *Always do right! This will gratify some people and astonish the rest.*

736. President Richard Nixon.

737. James and Elizabeth Monroe.

738. Jackie Kennedy.

739. In 1926.

740. Because official visitors who had to wait here were said to be "cooling off."

741. When layers of paint were cleaned off during restoration work in the Reagan presidency.

742. The Red Room.

743. Seventy.

744. What sparked friction between White House staff and servants accompanying visiting British royalty?

745. Who sat in the cabinet room for his daily shave by a member of the household staff?

746. Who kept a snake in the White House?

747. Which president was wrapped in the Stars and Stripes and had his head resting on a copy of the Constitution at his funeral?

748. How close was an assassin's bullet to President Reagan's heart after striking his rib and puncturing his lung?

749. What item of sentimental value did President Lyndon Johnson bring from Capitol Hill to his Oval Office?

750. Why was President Kennedy ordered onto a diet of bland food a year before he died?

751. When was the only time wine was served by President Rutherford Hayes and his wife, Lucy?

# ANSWERS

744. During the 1939 visit the royal servants criticized the food and demanded menus and a choice of food.

745. Theodore Roosevelt.

746. Archie Roosevelt, son of Theodore Roosevelt.

747. Andrew Jackson.

748. Less than an inch.

749. A desk with inlaid leather top which he had used as a U.S. Senator.

750. His doctor diagnosed a slight stomach disorder.

751. At a state dinner for Russian Grand Dukes Alexis and Constantin.

752. Why was President Eisenhower late in getting dressed for his inaugural celebrations?

753. When did Congress first grant funds to pay for White House clerks?

754. Which president got malaria in his final year in the White House?

755. How long had President Jefferson usually been up and working before receiving visitors at 9 a.m.?

756. Why didn't Abraham Lincoln drink liquor?

757. Who killed a man in a duel 23 years before he lived in the White House?

758. What did President McKinley's mother pray for the night before he went to live in the White House?

759. This president was so polite he got up and received visitors at his door rather than buzz his secretary to let them in.

760. Born Anne Frances Robbins, this first lady was known by her nickname.

# ANSWERS

752. He had left his white tie and tails in the train that brought him to Washington.

753. In 1857.

754. Franklin Pierce.

755. Four hours.

756. He told his secretary he did not like the taste of wine or spirits.

757. Andrew Jackson.

758. She said she prayed for her son to remain humble.

759. President Harry Truman.

760. Nancy Reagan's mother nicknamed her Nancy.

761. What code name did the Secret Service give President Richard Nixon?

762. What did President Ronald Reagan do while having his hair cut?

763. What was the president's pay in the final decade of the 20th century?

764. Why did President Franklin Roosevelt refuse to have the White House repainted when it was obviously in need of it?

765. What happened when President Kennedy opened the door to the Lincoln Bedroom for a viewing by visitors?

766. What made singer Sarah Vaughn cry at a State Dinner?

767. Which president invariably slept 11 hours every night and also took afternoon naps?

768. This president had four clocks on his Oval Office desk.

769. When was the fountain built on the north lawn?

# ANSWERS

761. Searchlight.

762. He watched movies on television.

763. $200,000 a year and $50,000 more for expenses.

764. He wanted to emphasize belt-tightening during World War 2.

765. He quickly closed it when he saw his mother asleep inside.

766. The black singer danced with the president and sang in the White House whereas 25 years earlier she said she could not book into city hotels.

767. Calvin Coolidge.

768. Harry Truman.

769. In 1873.

770. Link the trees below with the presidents who planted them.

   a) American Elm.
   b) Southern Magnolia.
   c) Scarlet Oak.
   d) White Oak.
   e) American Boxwood.
   f) Pin Oak.
   g) Saucer Magnolia.
   h) Willow Oak.
   i) Fern Leaf Beech.
   j) White Pine.
   k) Japanese Maple.
   l) Sugar Maple.
   m) Patmore Ash.
   n) Little Leaf Linden.

771. How high is the main building of the White House?

772. By what other name is the south lawn known?

773. Guess the total number of rooms.

774. How many rooms were added as a result of renovations and restoration work during the Truman presidency?

# ANSWERS

770. a) John Quincy Adams.
    b) Andrew Jackson
    c) Benjamin Harrison.
    d) Herbert Hoover.
    e) Harry Truman.
    f) Dwight Eisenhower.
    g) John F. Kennedy.
    h) Lyndon Johnson.
    i) Richard Nixon.
    j) Gerald Ford.
    k) Jimmy Carter.
    l) Ronald Reagan.
    m) George H.W. Bush.
    n) Bill Clinton.

771. 175 feet.

772. The President's Park.

773. There are 132 rooms.

774. Seven more rooms were created.

775. Who said nobody lives in the White House because occupants only "come and go."?

776. Which first lady scanned newspapers for bargain items and shopped by telephone?

777. This first lady got staff to sign pledges that they would not tattle on the first couple after leaving White House service.

778. Where was the first furnace installed?

779. What is the largest room in the White House?

780. When was the first telegraph installed?

781. Who acted as official hostess for the widower Andrew Jackson?

782. Name the tree planted on the grounds by President Grover Cleveland?

783. Where did Abraham Lincoln assemble his cabinet for regular meetings?

784. Where is the president's private movie theater?

# ANSWERS

775. President Calvin Coolidge.

776. Mamie Eisenhower.

777. Jackie Kennedy.

778. In the room now known as the Diplomatic Reception Room on the ground floor.

779. The East Room, which is 79 feet long and almost 37 feet wide.

780. In 1866.

781. His late wife's niece, Emily Donelson.

782. A Japanese Maple.

783. In the second floor room now called the Lincoln Bedroom.

Between the main building and the East Wing.